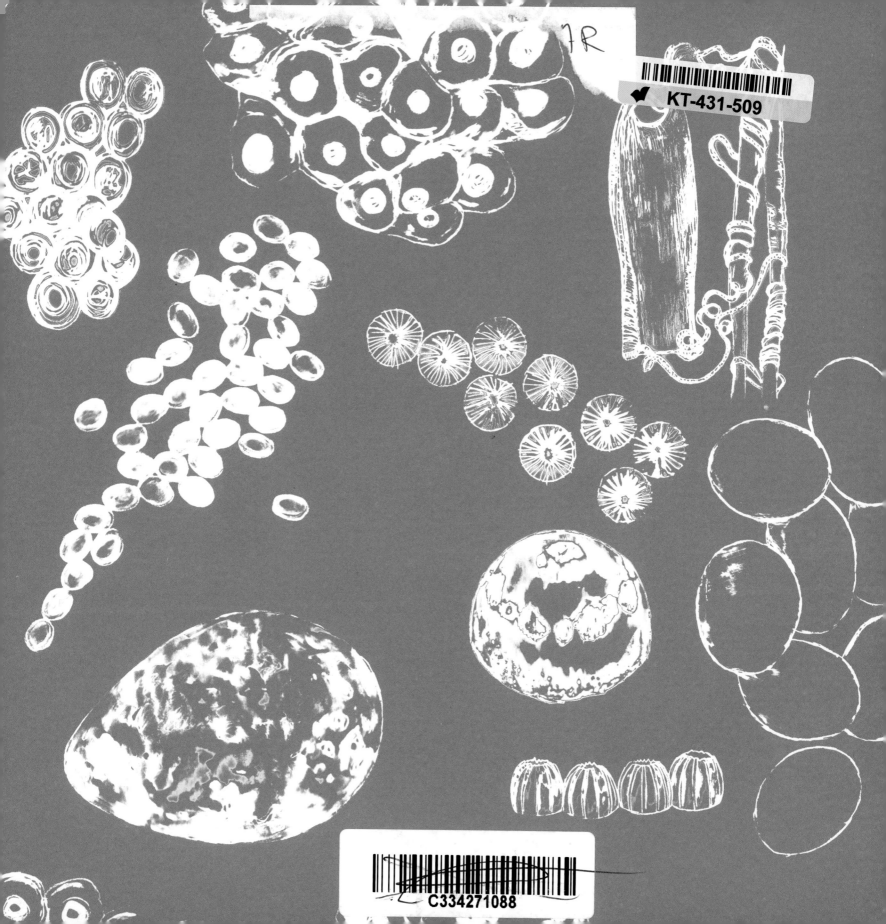

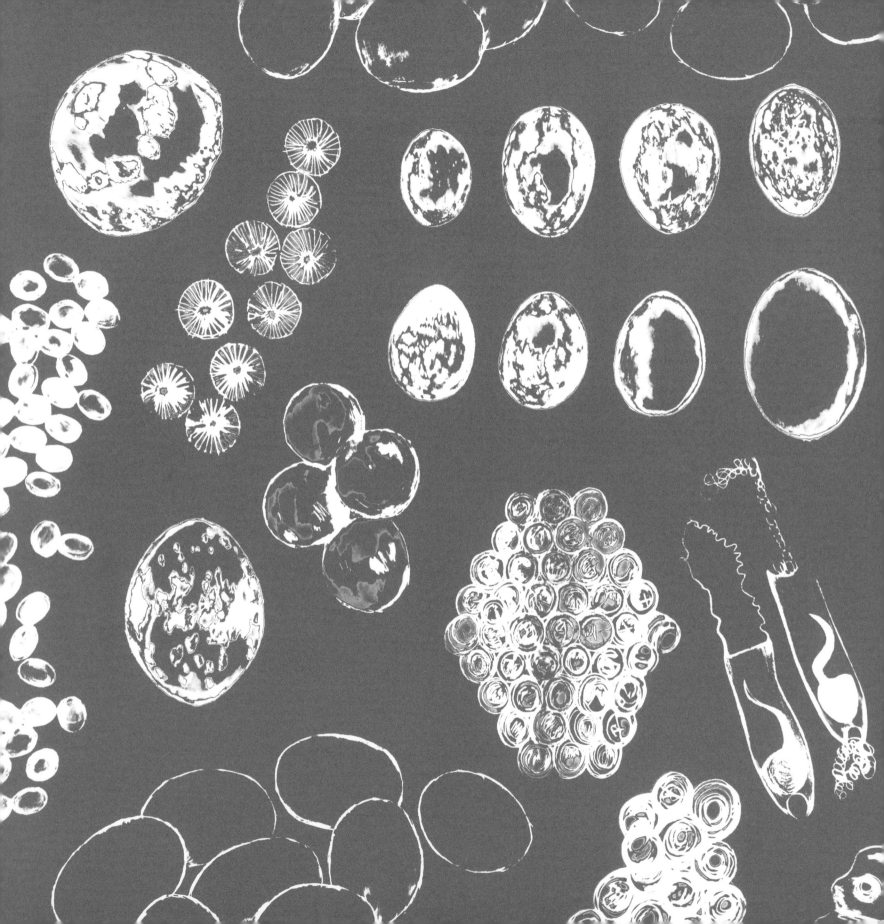

This book belongs to:

....

....

GRAFFEG

The Secret of the Egg
published by Graffeg 2018
© Copyright Graffeg 2018

Text © 2018 Nicola Davies.
Illustrations © 2018 Abbie Cameron.
Designed and produced by Graffeg.
www.graffeg.com

Graffeg Limited, 24 Stradey Park Business
Centre, Mwrwg Road, Llangennech, Llanelli,
Carmarthenshire SA14 8YP Wales UK
Tel 01554 824000 www.graffeg.com

The publisher gratefully acknowledges the
financial support of this book by the Welsh
Books Council www.gwales.com

ISBN 9781912213672

1 2 3 4 5 6 7 8 9

The Secret of the Egg

Written by
Nicola Davies

Illustrated by
Abbie Cameron

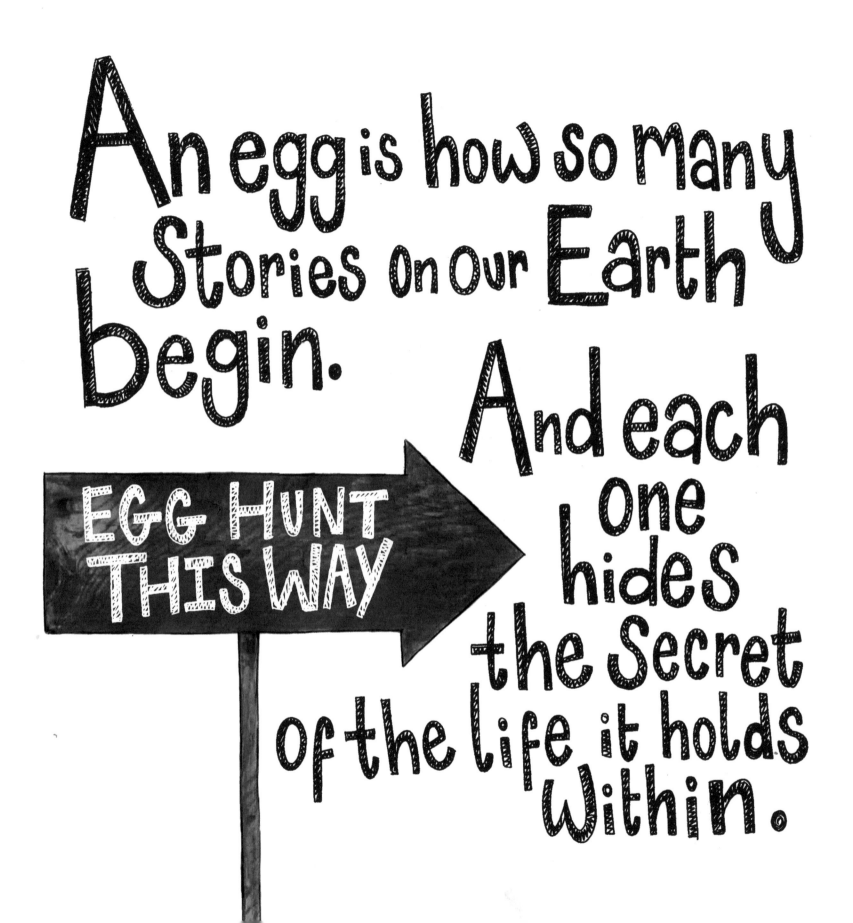

An egg is how so many Stories on our Earth begin.

And each one hides the Secret of the life it holds within.

EGG HUNT THIS WAY

It might be plain or speckled, red or white or blue,

Perhaps not even egg Shaped but like a fat Corkscrew.

It could be like a button,

Or Purse

Or melon pip,

It might be Squishy like a Jelly,

Or tougher than a Shoe,

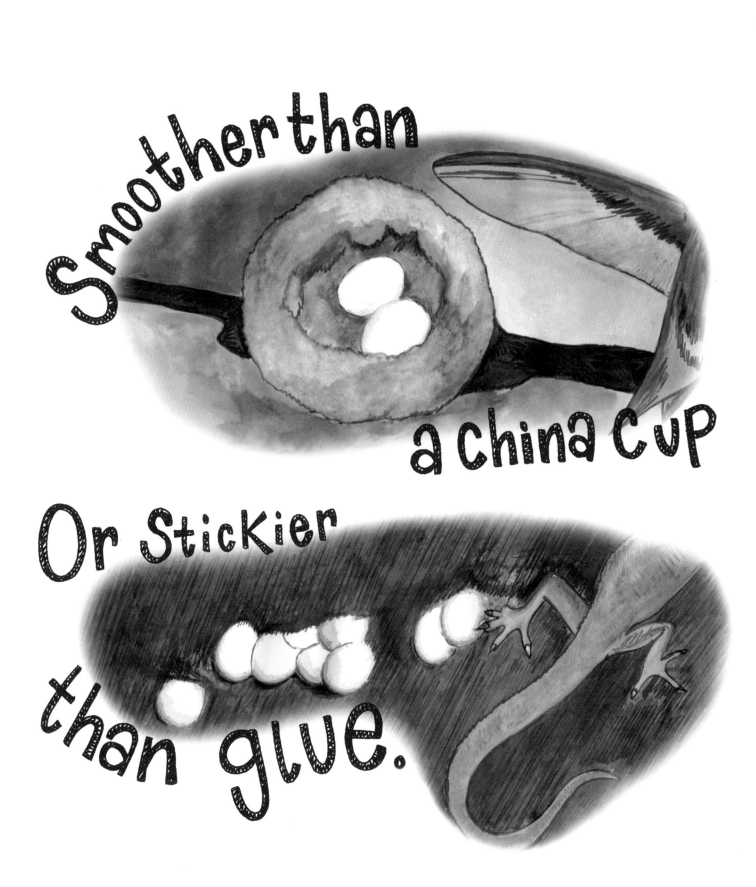

Smoother than a china cup

Or Stickier than glue.

Almost big enough for football

Or Smaller than
a pin,
No egg can
ever
tell you
What it
hides
Within.

An egg
might
be in a
puddle
that's high
up in a
tree,

Buried
underneath
the
Sand,

Or in the
big blue
Sea.

It might be safe inside a nest that's **Messy**

Or quite **neat**,

Or balanced on
its daddy's Very slowly
Shuffling feet.

It could be
cared for
carefully,

Or simply
left alone.

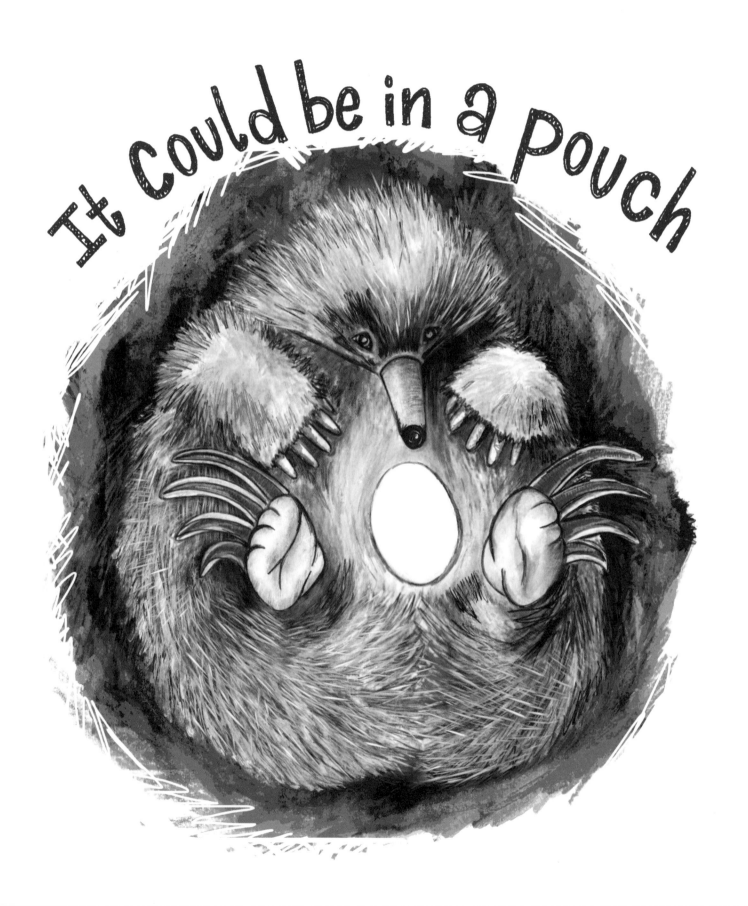

It could be in a pouch

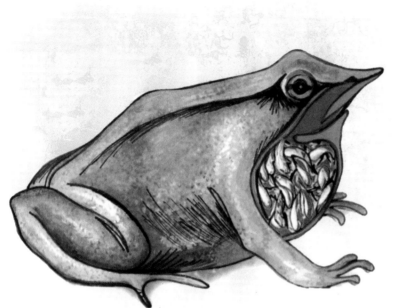

Or in a
mouth,

Or in a
tummy,
Belonging to
its daddy
not its ever
loving mummy.

For days,
or weeks,
or even
months,
eggs never
say a
word,

But at last
there comes a
day
when their
voices can
be heard.

A crick, a crack, a rip, a pop,

Now they no longer hide the Start of all those Stories that the egg held Safe inside.

PUZZLE TO FINISH

1

2

3

4

5

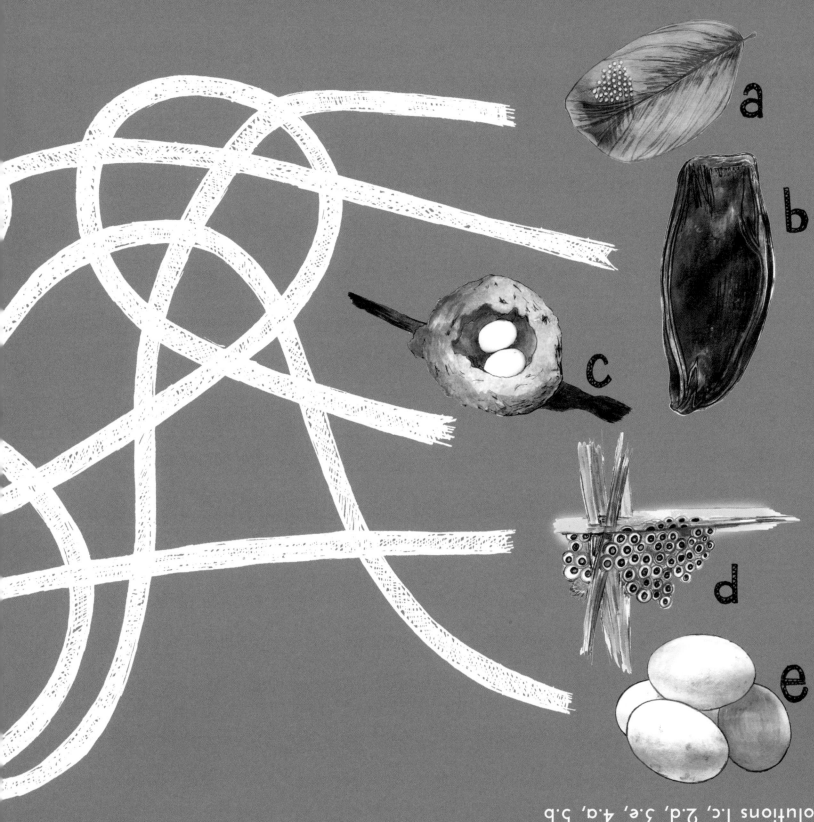

a

b

c

d

e

Nicola Davies

Nicola is an award-winning author, whose many books for children include *The Promise* (Green Earth Book Award 2015, CILIP Kate Greenaway Shortlist 2015), *Tiny* (AAAS Subaru Prize 2015), *A First Book of Nature*, *Whale Boy* (Blue Peter Award Shortlist 2014), and the *Heroes of the Wild* series (Portsmouth Book Prize 2014). She graduated in Zoology, studied whales and bats and then worked for the BBC Natural History Unit. Underlying all Nicola's writing is the belief that a relationship with nature is essential to every human being, and that now, more than ever, we need to renew that relationship. Nicola's children's books from Graffeg include *Perfect* (CILIP Kate Greenaway Longlist 2017), *The Pond* (CILIP Kate Greenaway Longlist 2018), the Shadows and Light series, *Animal Surprises*, *The Word Bird* and *Into the Blue*.

Abbie Cameron

Abbie Cameron was raised on the farmlands of the West Country. Surrounded by nature, she developed a love and appreciation for all creatures great and small. Abbie studied Illustration at University of Wales Trinity Saint David, where she first met Nicola Davies. Her style is playful and inventive, sharing some of the tongue-in-cheek attitude and doodle-like style of other contemporary British illustrators. She employs the use of bright colours and texture whilst playing with scale, composition and open space. Abbie's other books include *Animal Surprises* (The Klaus Flugge Prize for the Most Exciting Newcomer to Picture Book Illustration Longlist 2017), *The Word Bird* and *Into the Blue*, as well as their companion series of How to Draw books. Abbie was also highly commended in the Penguin Random House Design Awards 2014.

Rhyming Book Series

Discover the delights of nature with Zoologist and top children's author Nicola Davies. Follow the young adventurer as she treks through the jungle in *Animal Surprises*, dives deep down into the sea in *Into the Blue* and climbs up high into the trees in *The Word Bird*. All three rhyming books are fully illustrated in colour by Abbie Cameron.

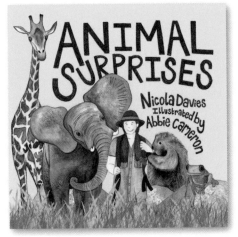

Animal Surprises
ISBN 9781910862445

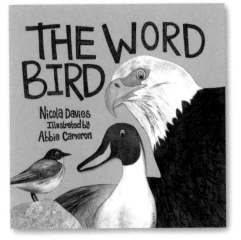

The Word Bird
ISBN 9781910862438

Current titles in the series:
- Animal Surprises
- The Word Bird
- Into the Blue
- The Secret of the Egg

Forthcoming titles:
- Invertebrates are Cool
- The Versatile Reptile

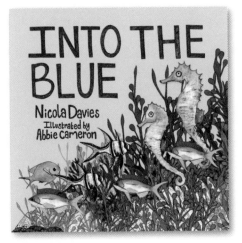

Into the Blue
ISBN 9781910862452

The Secret of the Egg
ISBN 9781912213672

GRAFFEG
www.graffeg.com

How to Draw Series

In this companion series, Abbie Cameron teaches children how to draw their favourite animals from the rhyming books step-by-step, alongside informative text about each species from Nicola Davies.

Titles in the series:

- Animal Surprises: How to Draw
- The Word Bird: How to Draw
- Into the Blue: How to Draw

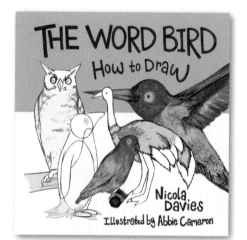

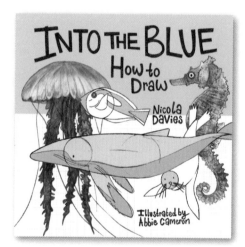

Animal Surprises: How to Draw
ISBN 9781912050567

The Word Bird: How to Draw
ISBN 9781912050574

Into the Blue: How to Draw
ISBN 9781912050550

Visit **www.graffeg.com/howtodraw** to watch Abbie drawing some of the animals from the series with step by step instructions.

GRAFFEG
www.graffeg.com

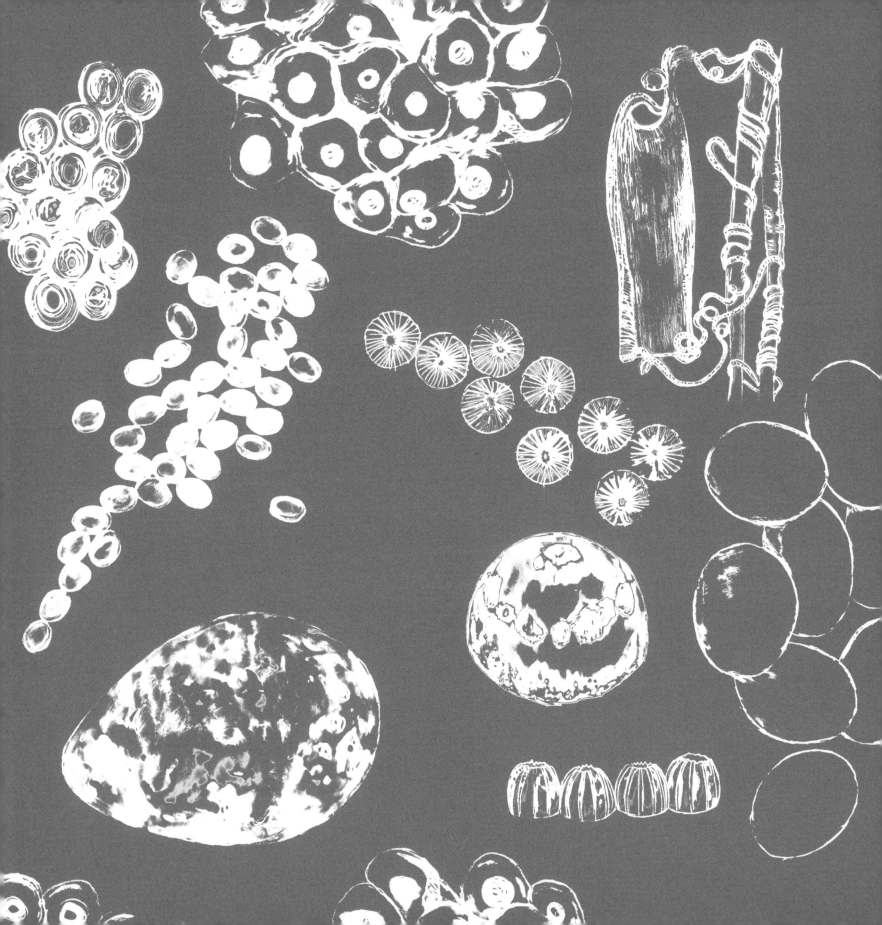

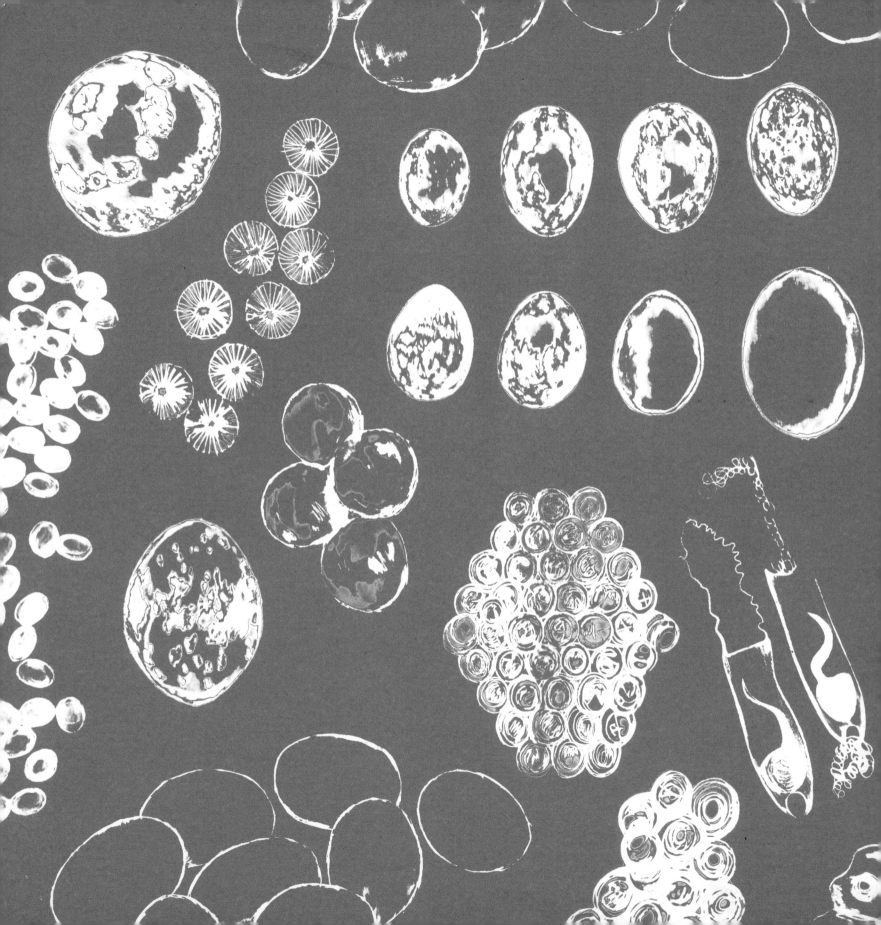